Running with the Lionhearted

Mary T. Wagner

WATERHORSE PRESS

OTHER CHILDREN'S BOOKS BY THIS AUTHOR

Finnigan the Circus Cat

Finnigan and the Lost Circus Wagon

Praise for
FINNIGAN THE CIRCUS CAT!!

"A charming animal story"

>Publishers Weekly

"An adorable story"

>Wishing Shelf Book Awards (U.K.)

"A heartwarming story about friendship, loyalty and the circus"

>White Tops Magazine

"A delightful read"

>Readers' Favorites

"Lots of good old fashioned fun"

>Good Books for Young Souls

Finnigan the Lionhearted

Copyright © 2020 by Mary T. Wagner

All rights reserved. Published by Waterhorse Press LLC.

No part of this book may be used or reproduced by any means, graphic, electronic, or mechanical, including photocopying, recording, taping or by any information storage retrieval system without the written permission of the author except in the case of brief quotations embodied in critical articles and reviews.

The views expressed in this work are solely those of the author. This book is a work of fiction. Names, characters, places, and incidents are either the product of the author's imagination or are used fictitiously, and any resemblance to actual persons, living or dead, business establishments, events, or locales is entirely coincidental.

Interior illustrations by the author.

First edition published December 4, 2020

ISBN: 978-0-578-80854-3

Visit the author's website at

www.marywagner.com

Contents

Prologue 1

One	Circus Tidings!	 4
Two	From Here to There	.. 10
Three	On the Road	 21
Four	Parting Ways	 27
Five	The Midway	 34
Six	The Fun House	 45
Seven	Tiny	 50
Eight	The Lions' Den	 65
Nine	Opposites Attract	 79
Ten	Anticipation!!	 91
Eleven	Under the Big Top!	... 97
Twelve	The Show Begins!	.. 106
Thirteen	Intermission	 115
Fourteen	Fright in Flight	 128
Fifteen	A Surprise Finale!	... 140

About the Author 160

For my very newest grandchildren

Eleanor and William,

And my wonderful grand-kitties

Linus and Mookah!!

Prologue

LITTLE LIONS

I've heard that cats—house cats, barn cats, farm cats and yes, even tiny kittens—are really just itsy bitsy models of the big cats like lions and tigers and panthers. You know, the ones with enormous teeth, and roars that can make the ground shake.

I think about that sometimes when I see Finnigan napping in the barn. He'll be snoozing in a warm patch of sunlight, with Leroy snuggled up in the crook of his arm. And then he'll stretch and he'll yawn, and all those sharp teeth will gleam in the sunlight before he closes his mouth again and looks all cuddly as a bunny.

Finnigan's certainly got the same kind of equipment as those big cats—the teeth for one thing, and those sharp claws—even if he doesn't roar. Leroy and I are just lucky that Finnigan thinks of us as family instead of dinner!

Oh, but please forgive my manners! I'm Maximillian—Max, for short—and I am a circus mouse. I live here at the Farnsworth Circus Museum in Beechville, Wisconsin with my cousin Leroy. And

Finnigan, of course.

Leroy and I were both born here. Our family has been living here for more years than you could count on two hands...or even four paws. You could say that circus is in our blood.

Finnigan joined us when he was just a tiny kitten, barely as big as Leroy. Since then he's grown much bigger, and some parts—like his legs and his tail—grew even more than we expected!

But if you ask me and Leroy, the biggest part of Finnigan has to be his heart. Like my Grandma Mabel always said, sometimes the biggest hearts come in the smallest packages.

And...oh my gosh! Everything else is going to have to wait until later, because we just found out that the circus is coming to town!

Chapter One

CIRCUS TIDINGS!!

Leroy just couldn't wait for Finnigan to wake up to tell him the good news. He was quivering with excitement, and believe me, when Leroy quivers, you want to step aside.

"The circus is coming!" he shouted as

he tugged on Finnigan's ear. "The circus is coming!"

Finnigan opened one eye but otherwise didn't move a whisker. The three of us were up in the loft of the Farnsworth Circus Museum. That's where where we all live and where we spend a lot of time staying out of sight of just about everybody.

Finnigan, of course, since he's not supposed to be there at all. That's been the rule since Lucy Farnsworth found him as a wee, wet kitten and brought him home. Her dad, Fred, is very allergic to cats. Leroy and I have been helping since the beginning, of course.

So far, Lucy is the only member of the family who could spill the beans on this big secret, but of course she won't.

But that little brother of hers, Mikey,

is going to cause trouble one of these days when he finally learns to talk.

Leroy and I also keep a very low profile as well because, of course, we're mice. For some strange reason, people just don't seem to really appreciate mice.

When we were growing up, we all heard that awful story about the Three Blind Mice and what happened to **them** when some farmer's wife found them in her kitchen. Just thinking about it still makes me shudder and my tail starts twitching. Somebody should have been arrested!!

So we try very hard to stay out of sight. Even Lucy, who is the whole reason that Finnigan is even here, doesn't know about us. Mikey...well that's a different story. He's seen us and he's been trying to say the word "mouse" for quite a while now. We won't be in the clear forever.

But until then, we have our ways of getting around and into the house that involve doors, and porches, and things that the Farnsworths think are locked up tight against the wind and the cold.

Which is how we just happened to be sitting outside the Farnsworth kitchen this morning when Fred got a surprise phone call about the circus coming to town.

Most mornings, the routine involves Leroy and me sneaking into the house. Then we wait just outside the kitchen to grab any breakfast leftovers. It's not foolproof, but it's a system.

Boomer, the family dog, was lying next to Mikey's chair, hoping that some of the little guy's pancakes would go flying and be considered "free range."

Boomer, being a dog, is a natural optimist, and edged himself so close to Mikey that his head was resting right under the chair. Any pancake pieces that fell would probably not even hit the floor.

So when Fred broke the news to the family, the kids shouted, Shirley clapped, and Boomer sprang to his feet and clunked his head against the chair.

Leroy was so excited he started to dance a joyful jig.

"Hey," I said, slapping him on the shoulder, "we're supposed to be **incognito!**" He quickly flatted himself against the wall again and kicked his tail out of sight.

"Sorry Max," he whispered, but I could still feel his excitement. And I felt like I'd just been zapped by a giant spark of electricity. I leaned closer to hear the rest of the details. And why, you ask, were we so excited?

Because for the first time ever in our lives, ***the real circus was coming to Beechville!!!***

Chapter Two

FROM HERE TO THERE

Finnigan's other eye snapped open. He yawned and stretched all the way from his nose to the tip of his tail. In Finnigan's case, this is a very long way. Then he snuggled himself back into a warm cat ball in the sunshine where we'd found him.

He shook his head as he eyed Leroy, who was still trembling with excitement.

"The circus," he said. "The real circus?"

Leroy nodded and then tried to do a cartwheel to shake off some of that extra energy. He landed on his butt with a "whump" and a flurry of dust. Little pieces of straw stuck to his whiskers and he worked at batting them off.

I told Finnigan what we'd heard. Yes indeed, the Spence-Haywaller tent circus was going to be rolling in to Beechville ***later today!!***

This news had come as a surprise to everyone. But the fairgrounds in the town ten miles over where the circus was supposed to play were flooded. And so the Beechville fairgrounds became a perfect solution.

Finnigan looked around the barn with its circus wagons in the center ring, and the old posters of fantastical mermaids and leaping lions and trapeze artists soaring above strings of elephants, and, of course, the old cannon...and smiled so wide you could see his back teeth. That is ***very*** far in a cat smile if you think about it!

He suddenly sat up straight. "Will there be lions?" he asked. His green eyes twinkled with excitement.

"Oh yes, lions!" Leroy squealed, clapping his hands together.

"And tigers!" I added.

"And dancing bears!" Leroy threw in for good measure.

"Maybe," I said.

"Do you think we could meet them?" Finnigan asked, and a rolling purr began to fill the space around us. I've noticed that this happens when he's super happy. The things you learn from living with a cat!

"I don't see why not," I said. I sensed where Finnigan's mind was going with all this. There were posters in the barn that showed the "big cats" in all their growling, leaping, roaring glory, jumping through flaming hoops and balancing on each other's backs to form astonishing piles of teeth and claws.

The looked like they could never be scared by **anything!** Finnigan had grown up here with those pictures in his head, along with the magnificent gold lions on the King of Beasts wagon downstairs.

Finnigan leaped from the loft to the trapeze hanging from the roof, and swung himself to the other side and back again.

Then he jumped to the top of the Snake Charmer wagon just as Fred and Shirley, along with Charlie and Lucy, swung the doors of the barn open. Mikey stayed outside, riding his tricycle in circles.

Finnigan jumped off the top of the wagon like greased lightning, and picked a hiding spot behind the costume trunk. Fred strode around the wagons like a ringmaster eyeing up a line of elephants, checking that trunks and tails were in order right before the show started.

"I think a lot of people will be driving past here because of the Spence-Haywaller circus," he said. "We should push some of these wagons into the yard so they can see them as they drive by."

Shirley sipped her coffee. "This one for sure," she said, pointing at the King of Beasts. That one, with its snarling lions and tigers painted in gold against a bright red background, had always been Finnigan's favorite, of course.

"And the Snake Charmer," Charlie chimed in. With its coiling cobras, glittering glass eyes and ivory fangs, it had always given me and Leroy the creeps. But little kids seemed to **love** it!

"And the calliope," Fred added. He and Charlie both rolled up their sleeves, and in a few minutes the barn was emptier by three wagons and once again we had the place to ourselves.

"That was close," Finnigan said.

"Good thing Mikey didn't come in," added Leroy, who'd finally gotten his whiskers and fur all back in order. "That little guy is nothing but trouble," he said with a shake of his head.

This whole act of pretending that the

three of us don't really live here is getting harder and harder! Finnigan has to stay under the radar because of Fred's cat allergy, and Leroy and me...well, like I said, people don't often try to make friends with mice.

"You know we'll have to go," said Finnigan, with a note of newfound authority in his voice.

"I don't want to leave," said Leroy with a note of sadness. "We grew up here, you know."

I often can't figure out where Leroy's mind runs to sometimes, and this was one of those times. I cuffed him on the ear, just enough to get his attention.

"Go to the circus, you ***goose***," I said.

"OH," he said and settled back into a comfortable slouch. A smile spread across his face as he began to contemplate this new adventure. "How are we going to get there?"

That was a really good question. Suddenly the distance from the Farnsworth Circus Museum to the fairgrounds on the other side of town seemed as far as going to the moon.

After all, the barn and the house and the yard around it **was** our whole world. We'd never gone farther than the stream that ran behind the house. And even then we were looking over our shoulders. You can't be too careful when you're a mouse.

"You can ride with me," said Finnigan. "I'll make like a camel and you can be my passengers." Then he went back to leaping around the barn for exercise and amusement. The distance between the rest of the wagons had doubled now that three of them were outside, and it made for some spectacular "air time" on Finnigan's part.

While the circus wasn't expected to perform until the next day, we knew that the trucks carrying the performers and all the supplies would be rolling in to town today to set up. So by mid-afternoon we all squeaked out of the barn to start our journey.

Boomer intercepted us at the edge of the yard. Now Boomer is a dog who doesn't say much, but his big brown eyes clearly pleaded "can I come too?"

It took just about a second for the three of us to lock eyes, and then our caravan added one big yellow dog.

After a few strides of bouncing around on Finnigan's shoulder blades, it was clear we needed a new ride share plan.

"What?" Finnigan said with a scowl.

"My fur's not soft enough? It's not like I'm a porcupine or something."

"Your shoulder blades are kind of bony," said Leroy with an embarrassed shrug. We climbed down from a sulking Finnigan and picked more comfortable seats on Boomer's broad back.

Then our oddball caravan resumed, and I settled back for the ride. It made perfect sense for all of us critters to take this chance for an early circus viewing. Because if the whole Farnsworth family decided to see the circus together the next day—and good grief, why wouldn't they!—Boomer would surely be left behind to "guard the house."

The Farnsworths didn't realize that guarding the place was really a team effort. But there's a lot that people don't know.

And what the Farnsworths didn't know about us could fill a circus tent.

Chapter Three

ON THE ROAD

Boomer led the parade. He was the only one of us who had actually been any distance away from the Farnsworth Circus Museum. He always seemed a bit sore and grumpy after those trips into town, and I'd heard

Shirley say the word "vet-er-in-a-ri-an" a couple of times regarding these jaunts.

But Boomer must have been looking out the windows while they drove because it sure seemed like he knew where he was going.

Leroy's eyes were as big as buttons with excitement. We pitched and swayed, rolling on Boomer's big shoulders like we were on a raft in the ocean. Once we were out of sight of the barn, Boomer took what looked like a narrow deer path through a stretch of tall grass. It came up to his chin, and the tassels of grass, heavy with seeds, whipped Leroy and me as we passed.

"That tickles!" Leroy laughed. Maybe it tickled Leroy—he's so much bigger—but for me, it felt more like being pounded with a giant noodle. But still, the view was amazing!

Finnigan brought up the rear. Mostly, when we looked behind us, the grass had already swayed back into place and so all we could see was the white tip of his tail.

Leroy's imagination started to grow on me. I began to picture Boomer as an elephant, and Leroy and me as a pair of maharajas in India at least a hundred years ago. We were riding in a howdah and scanning the horizon for tigers as our giant beast of burden parted the grasslands. Leroy smiled when I told him as much, especially when I mentioned the part about looking for tigers.

"Oh, I thought I saw one over there," he said, and pointed to our right.

"What?" I said, and I suddenly sat up straighter. I didn't see anything but grass ...and some colorful pennants fluttering in the distance. The fairgrounds must be getting closer!

"It was just for a second," he said with a frown, now looking over to our left. "I thought I saw a tiger's tail twitching in the grass."

I opened my mouth to say "don't be ridiculous" and then I remembered that the last time Leroy thought he saw a tiger …he did.

I peered again in the same direction. I only saw the tops of the grasses waving back and forth like Shirley's white sheets hanging on the clothesline. I tried to focus harder. Was that a shadow that I saw? A ripple in the grass that looked out of place? It was impossible to tell.

Oh, my mood suddenly went from happy to scared, and my stomach did three somersaults before it settled back into place, still with a queasy feeling.

Tigers, I knew, were not really the problem. At least not here. We weren't really sitting in a howdah on an elephant during a tiger hunt. There were no tigers in Beechville, Wisconsin unless they were pacing in their cages at the fairgrounds.

But what Beechville ***did*** have were two pampered and thoroughly wicked house cats named Hector and Godfrey who lived just down the street from the Farnsworths.

And while they had the regular, normal cat appetites for mice, it drove them positively bonkers to know that Finnigan and Leroy and I considered ourselves a little circus family.

I think they considered Finnigan a traitor to the glorious cat cause. Making a meal someday out of me and Leroy was not only featured on their menu, it was a matter of solemn principle.

I kept my thoughts to myself. Leroy's worries had already evaporated and he was back to having too good of a time to spoil it. And besides, look who we had with us for protection!

Finnigan had already saved Leroy from becoming a cat lunch months ago, and Boomer thought chasing both Hector and Godfrey into bramble bushes was a very fine sport.

No, I told myself as I tried to get my nervous stomach to behave, we were in absolutely no danger at all.

Chapter Four

PARTING WAYS

The Spence-Haywaller Circus must have pulled into Beechville before dawn, because by the time we got there, set-up was in full swing.

At the far end of the fairgrounds, the tent poles were standing tall while the canvas roof and sides were being carefully hauled up into place.

And the Midway was unfolding in front of our very eyes.

"Would you look at that," said Finnigan. Boomer sat his haunches down, and Leroy and I slid down his back. All four of us stared at a sight we never thought we would see in our lifetimes.

There were rides—from a mechanical Giant Ferris Wheel to a circle of real ponies wearing little saddles and halters, quietly munching their alfalfa hay in a little paddock and waiting for some pint-sized customers to come along.

A Tilt-A-Whirl was getting safety-checked, with long rolling rumbles as the chairs swung around and then slowed, then swung into new circles again. A little farther on, there was a kids' airplane ride, with little planes attached to skinny metal beams, that "flew" when the whole contraption turned on the center pole.

Puffs of dust kicked up from a line of elephants. Horses whinnied in the distance. Metal tent poles clanged, colorful pennants fluttered in the wind, and canvas tent walls snapped and boomed in the breeze.

It was almost too much to take in at once. Sort of like hearing the story of Jack and the Beanstalk every night before bed, and then suddenly waking up one morning to find that you're in the giant's castle!

"I want to find the lions," said Finnigan.

"I want to see the elephants," said Leroy, clapping his paws in excitement.

I wanted to see the Fun House myself, but I figured I'd better work on keeping this herd together first.

Boomer didn't say anything, as usual, but took two deep doggy sniffs and then suddenly trotted away like he had someplace to go. It probably involved other dogs, I figured. I hoped he wouldn't get his heart broken by some fancy French Poodle who was just in town for the show.

Finnigan shrugged as Boomer disappeared, his big yellow tail wagging like a metronome, into the kaleidoscopic scene.

"The elephants," Leroy said again, as he looked around the yard.

From far left came the unmistakable roar of a big cat, and suddenly every hair on Finnigan stood up straight.

"Hear that?" he asked.

How could we possibly miss it, I wondered.

Without a second's hesitation, Finnigan dashed off, leaving just little dust whirls in the gravel as his long legs took him in leaps and bounds closer to meeting his heroes.

Then from the far right an elephant bugled and Leroy jumped for joy. He looked around and then back at me, and grabbed my hand.

"Max, it's the elephants," he said. "We've got to see the elephants!"

There was no use arguing. For one thing, Leroy is much bigger, so if he wanted to he could carry me over his shoulder anywhere he pleased. For another, he's my first cousin, and until Finnigan showed up, Leroy was the only close family I had!

And for the third thing, well…really… I'm the one with the most common sense in the family. You will not catch me being needlessly brave, taking risks, or trusting fate. I'm a mouse and I know it!

When it comes to the food chain, mice are pretty close to the bottom, although I suppose earthworms might be one step lower. Snakes think we're tasty, owls are always trouble, and cats—***especially cats***—are well known for liking to "play with their food." Finnigan is the exception, of course.

So when it comes to being a mouse and staying alive, especially anywhere outside of the circus museum, Leroy definitely would need my help.

So, it was off to find the elephants. My conscience tugged at me just a little.

Since Finnigan had shown up, the three of us had been an inseparable team. We really should all be sticking together. As they say, there's safety in numbers.

But then again, I decided to try to be an optimist for once. Leroy and I were just two little mice. We'd be practically invisible amidst all this glorious activity and colorful chaos.

Really, without Finnigan and Boomer along, what could possibly go wrong?

Chapter Five

THE MIDWAY

Once we had decided to go find the elephants, it seemed that everything else suddenly got Leroy's attention.

"Max, look!" he squealed, and pointed. "They're unloading the horses!!"

I looked up just in time to see a giraffe's foot pass over our heads, and I yanked Leroy sideways. We both tumbled into a pile of loose hay as a giant tower of big spots and long legs and rubbery lips lurched past.

"That was close," he said nervously, and scratched the top of his head.

"No kidding," I said. "I guess we should look up a little bit more."

"Uh Max," he said, and his eyes were big with alarm. "Turn around right now."

"Seriously?" I said. Our close call had already passed. And then I felt something soft and rubbery nudge my shoulder while my tail started to lift off the ground ...with me still attached.

Leroy hit me with a flying tackle, and my tail came free just as the giraffe yanked a mouth full of alfalfa and kept on walking. It figured. With a neck that long, those lips could still be grabbing food that was already behind him.

"Thanks, pal," I said, but Leroy had already spied the Carousel.

"Oh Max!" he said, and clapped his paws. "A Carousel! Wouldn't you love to ride on that?"

What's a cousin to say?

It seemed a very long way from where we sat to the Carousel under an open sky. Then again, it didn't seem like night-hunting owls were going to be a problem in the middle of the day in a busy place like this. And I hadn't seen any cats around. So we took a deep breath and we ran for it.

We were both out of breath by the time we got the shade under the Carousel's round platform. It felt as cool as an ice box, a good place for a little rest. Of course in two breaths Leroy was off "yondering" as he liked to call it, and hoisted himself up to the wooden floor.

I followed, naturally. Somebody's got to keep him out of trouble.

The Midway around us was an ocean of excitement. Roustabouts set up games and machines, acrobats stretched, and ponies and poodles and clowns and jugglers passed by without a glance in our direction. It was like we were in the eye of a hurricane.

"Holy Moley," Leroy said as he looked around. We were in a forest of shiny metal poles. Above us, a herd of fancy wooden horses of all colors pawed the air with their wooden hooves and whinnied through their big wooden teeth.

There were zebras and unicorns and

sea serpents and lions. There were white horses with blue manes, and brown horses with red and white manes like candy canes. They were all frozen in mid-gallop, waiting for someone to flip the "on" switch and start the music.

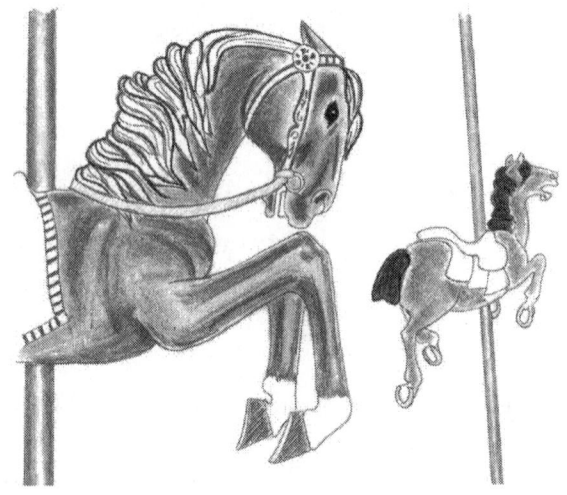

Someone had left a coiled rope on the platform. I saw Leroy's eyes fix on it and then follow it upward and across two of the magical steeds.

The words "we should keep going and

find the elephants" came out of my mouth about two seconds too late, and by the time "elephants" had gotten out of my throat Leroy was already up the rope and perched on the saddle horn of a bucking bronco. For a big fellow, he can move really fast when he wants to.

I ran up behind him, of course, and picked a perch between a unicorn's ears. The view from up here was even more amazing! After all, most of we see all the time is at ground level. Now, nearly everybody we saw looked shorter.

Except for the giraffes, of course. They still towered over everything.

Leroy patted the bronco's wooden mane and scooted up to the top of bridle. "His name should be 'Comanche' or 'Scout'," he said. "Something Western."

"What?"

"You remember the old movies," he said. "The classic Westerns."

"What?"

"Like 'Stagecoach' and 'High Noon'."

I stared at him.

"Back when Old Man Farnsworth was alive, and we watched TV with him in the evenings."

Now ***that*** I remembered, but barely. Most of what I recalled about those happy nights was snoozing with a full stomach in the fold of a torn sofa cushion, black and white pictures flashing on the screen as I fell asleep. I'm absolutely positive that Old Man Farnsworth had no idea that we were there.

Leroy closed his eyes, and blissfully imagined he was in one of those movies, driving a herd of cattle across the Plains. "I can feel that prairie wind in my face," he said, holding the edge of the leather bridle. "It's just like we're there!"

I hated to break it to him, but I felt the unicorn start to circle forward. We **were** moving. One of the workers had been checking the machines one at a time, and now the Carousel's time was up.

I held on to the back of the unicorn's bridle more tightly. Leather straps gave a better grip than those polished ears. The horses moved up and down, up and down, in circles, picking up speed.

I finally picked an instant when our two saddles were nearly even, and ran over to Leroy's steed. I reached the saddle. Leroy was now wobbling above me, still on the bronco's ears. Balancing has never been his strong suit, and this ride was proving too much to handle.

"Give me your hand!" I said, and reached toward him.

His fingers were curled in a death grip on the leather strap. "I can't," he said, as he slowly started to slip a little more sideways.

I inched closer, and put one paw on top of his. "Come on, Leroy, grab on," I shouted. "I'll help pull you up."

"I...just...***can't***..." he said and he began to slide downward in slow motion.

Centrifugal force had just about peeled Leroy off the bridle. He was starting to slide down the bronco's shiny shoulder when suddenly a blur of grey and white flew past, snatching Leroy up by the scruff of his neck as the Carousel animals moved up and down like pistons.

I ran down the rope as Finnigan was spitting out some extra mouse hair. Leroy sat beside him, looking dazed but otherwise fine.

"I just had a feeling that this place might be a little too big for you, and came back to offer a ride again," he said. Leroy gave Finnigan a big hug.

"It's like you had ESP or something," he said. "We really *are* a family!"

"Sure, that has to be it," Finnigan said. "Now let's go."

While Leroy was climbing up to his skinny shoulder, Finnigan leaned his head down to my ear. In a whisper, he said that he'd been half way to the lion's tent when he thought he caught a whiff of Hector and Godfrey and figured he'd better turn around.

"Seems like my timing was right either way."

I shuddered at the possibilities, but

decided to not share them with Leroy. At least **one** of us could still be carefree at the circus!

"Climb aboard," Finnigan said, and once again we took our seats like maharajas.

Chapter Six

THE FUN HOUSE

Of course bouncing on Finnigan's skinny shoulder blades was nothing like riding on Boomer's broad back, so it wasn't long before we skipped riding in favor of walking.

Finnigan rolled his eyes. "You *know*

we'll get there faster if you ride," he said.

I just shrugged. I was standing still but my butt felt like it was still bouncing.

"It's this way to the lions," Finnigan said.

"But I can still hear the elephants over there," Leroy replied, pointing in the other direction and leaning his whole self into it.

I looked at Finnigan and shrugged again. Following Leroy had clearly become our "new normal," so we reset our course to Elephant Central.

By now it was obvious that the safest way isn't always the shortest way, so we ducked into the Fun House to keep under cover.

The lights were dim and mysterious, and Finnigan took the lead. His cat's eyes reflected a bright emerald green.

Every few feet, we just had to stop and stare. A baby hippo sat in a tank of water, blowing bubbles with his nose. Two screeching chimps beckoned for us to join them in their cage. Leroy looked over his shoulder at me as if to say "How about it?" but I shook my head.

We all ran as fast as we could past the glass box with the boa constrictor inside. He followed us with those creepy eyes and flicking tongue from one side of the case to the other. Then we scooted behind a clown lacing up his giant red shoes.

Finnigan stopped suddenly. Leroy ran into his tail. I ran into Leroy.

"What's up?" I asked while I worked the kinks out of my whiskers. Finnigan and Leroy started laughing at the same time. I turned to see the reflections of all three of us in a set of mirrors, but these were the strangest mirrors I'd ever seen.

I stared at myself in amazement. I looked...***huge!*** My ears were big. My nose was big. My tummy was big. I looked like ...***Leroy!***

I looked over at Leroy, who was staring at his own reflection. He was... ***tiny!*** His ears were tiny. His nose was tiny. His tummy was tiny. He looked like ...***me!***

Finnigan could hardly stop laughing when he saw us. Leroy stared at his own reflection in awe.

"I always wondered what it would be like to be little," he said. I pondered the switch for a minute. My conscience gave a little twitch for having made so many jokes about Leroy's giant size before this.

Then I looked over at Finnigan's

reflection. The transformation was magical. Absolutely ***everything*** was shorter in all directions! Those long legs, the rope-like tail, his narrow face…he looked like a tiny kitten again!

"What!" he said as Leroy and I burst into giggles at the same time. "What's so funny?"

Leroy pointed and Finnigan finally took a look at himself in the mirror. As he moved this way and that out of the "sweet spot," parts of him grew long again—an arm, a leg, just the tail.

If he moved just right in front of the mirror, it was like we had a brand new kitten with us all over again.

Chapter Seven

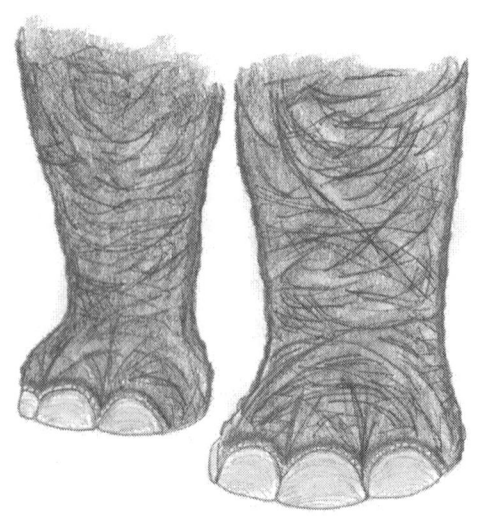

TINY

We ducked out of the Fun House just as a line of elephants walked past. We could hardly believe our eyes.

They were as big as houses! Or at least bigger than the Farnsworths' minivan. And they were definitely bigger than some of our circus wagons.

"Holy Moley," said Finnigan. Leroy was absolutely speechless. His mouth was open in shock but no words came out.

The line of elephants stopped, and we shrank back against the Fun House wall. Giant squishy feet shifted their weight from one leg to the other. They were like giant puddles of grey with soft, curvy edges. Their toenails were bigger than Leroy.

We all let our eyes travel up-up-up, from the feet like giant ottomans to the legs like big tree trunks, to the massive, humongous shoulders and bellies. Everything was covered with brownish grey, wrinkled leather. Even the wrinkles had wrinkles!

At the top of these moving mountains, huge ears flapped like sails. One of the elephants at the front of the line picked up a trunk full of dust and threw it over his back. The dust particles drifted in our direction, and Leroy sneezed.

"Kerchew!!

"Shhh..." I hissed. "Do you want them to know we're here?" I mean, really, who knew if elephants liked the taste of mice as a garnish?

Finnigan eyed us both. "Seriously?" he said. "Sometimes even *I* can hardly hear you."

That's all Leroy needed to know, and he edged a little closer. The nearest elephant dropped the end of its trunk to the ground, and it landed at our feet with a soft "thud."

The line didn't seem to be in any

hurry to get moving, and after a little while Finnigan started to lose interest and began to glance around. From somewhere nearby came the throaty cough of a big cat, and his ears perked up again.

"This way fellas," he said. "You've seen the elephants, so let's go!" He turned away and started walking toward the sound of the big cats as though he was hypnotized, and expecting us to fall into line behind him again.

Leroy, on the other hand, was mesmerized by the pachyderm snout sitting in front of him.

The rest of the trunk waved back and forth ever so slightly, like a snake hanging from a tree, but the rubbery end touching the ground barely moved at all.

Leroy moved closer, like he wanted to

touch it. I tugged on his tail, his lovely fur-covered, mousey, pride-and-joy tail.

"Hey," he said but yanked his hand back. "What was that for?"

I pointed upwards to the gigantic pile of wrinkled grey skin and muscle and white tusks that stood out like dead tree branches. "There is absolutely **no percentage** in tickling an elephant, you ninny!"

"Max, you worry too much," he said, and resumed tempting fate. "Check out these feet! I'm sure he won't even feel this!"

One of those feet was right in front of him, and Leroy knocked on a giant toenail like it was a door. He was right. Nothing moved, not even a twitch. I looked over at Finnigan for a little backup, but all I could see was the white tip of his tail disappearing in the distance as he resumed his search for the big cats.

I turned back to Leroy just in time to see a blur of grey and orange flash by us like a whip. But instead of a "crack," the sound that followed was a loud "whump."

We rubbernecked it as a large, fluffy pile of orange and cream striped bad intentions slid down the canvas wall of the tent next door and disappeared behind a bin of oats.

It was Godfrey, one half of that evil pair of mouse-hating cats. Finnigan's nose hadn't been wrong! But what the heck had just happened?

"Did you see that?" I scratched my head. But instead of Leroy beside me, there was just empty space.

The end of that elephant trunk he'd so admired was now wrapped around

Leroy, and it whisked him suddenly to the very top of that wrinkled mountain.

The trunk gently deposited Leroy between those giant ears. I tried to hide. No such luck. Before I could move and get my whole self out of sight, I felt my own tail caught by what felt like a soft pair of tweezers, and suddenly I was airborne.

My life flashed before my eyes. It was pretty short and dull, right up until the part where Finnigan had shown up. Then, in the next instant, I was plopped down next to Leroy, who sat with a contented grin on his face.

"Pretty wild, Max, huh?" he said. "Can we keep him? He seems friendly, and I'm sure there's room in the barn."

Right then, I wasn't moving a muscle except for my eyeballs. Those worked just fine.

We could see in all directions. The Big Top was nearly up. A string of horses went prancing past, their hooves kicking up little poofs of dust. The airplane ride started up, and a half dozen little planes with propellers swung in a circle.

Of more immediate importance, I saw the tip of Godfrey's fluffy tail twitch a little from behind the grain bin. It was going to take him a while before he felt like moving, I was sure. But that meant Hector was still around here somewhere!

The rubbery nose suddenly presented itself next to us. The nostrils were big enough for me to walk into, not that I wanted to try doing that!

"I think he wants us to get on," said Leroy, and he grabbed my hand and pulled me along with him. There was no point in arguing. I couldn't think of another way to get off this mountain. The trunk lifted us from where we were sitting and floated us carefully to a steady perch on the edge of the Fun House roof.

Then our strange new friend turned to face us. His forehead was as big as Old Man Farnsworth's rocking chair. A big brown eye surrounded by grey cracks and wrinkles stared back at us.

"My name is Tiny," he said. "What's yours?"

I cleared my throat a couple of times and then found my voice again. "I'm Max," I said. "This is my cousin Leroy. What just happened?"

I already had a pretty good idea of the mechanics involved in hurling a large cat into a canvas wall, but the "why" was still missing.

"Well," said Tiny, "I saw that cat was

looking at you and I knew I had to do something."

"Why?" Leroy asked. His eyes were full of puzzlement. I was mystified myself. Circus families are pretty tight and filled with kindness, but until a minute ago, Tiny had been a total stranger.

"He was looking at you like the lions look at the horses when feeding time runs a little late," he said.

Oh boy. Leroy and I shivered in unison.

"What brings you to the circus?" our new friend asked.

"It's a long story," Leroy said.

"Well we're going to be here a long time," Tiny offered. "I heard there's a camel stuck in a chute up ahead, so we're going to be waiting like freight cars in a railroad yard."

Well then, the whole story came out. The royal physician for Mad King Ludwig. Our Great-Great-Great-Great Grandfather Felix who was the doctor's pet pocket mouse. The medical conference in Berlin, and then that impulsive dash toward the lights and excitement of a circus life so long ago.

"Wow," said Tiny. "And I thought you were just here for the food!"

"Food!" Leroy's ears perked up.

"Yes," said Tiny. "I like the peanuts, but I've heard that the popcorn is top notch."

"But what's your story?" I asked.

"I was born in this circus," Tiny said. "That's my mom at the head of the line," he said proudly.

"But why are you called 'Tiny'?"

"Well, as elephants go," he said "I'm a

lot shorter than the rest. At first they called me 'Freckles' because of the pink spots on my cheeks and my nose. But once I stopped growing, the circus owners decided to change it. I guess it made for better publicity."

We looked further up the line and realized that we were indeed in the company of the smallest mountain in this range. Who knew?

Finnigan reappeared. He had interrupted his search for the lions when he saw Godfrey fly through the air, and was sitting off to the side, slack-jawed with astonishment.

"Hey," said Tiny, "do you want to join your friends up here?"

Finnigan shook his head. Another roar from a giant cat in the distance brought us back to focus.

"You know, we really came here to see the lions," I said. "Can you help us out?"

"Why do you want to see those guys?" Tiny asked. "They're meat eaters, and if you haven't noticed, you are all made out of meat!"

"It's for our friend Finnigan over there," Leroy explained. "The one with the long tail."

Tiny pointed with his trunk toward a metal building beyond the Fun House. "That's where you'll find the lions," he said. "Though I don't know why you'd want to. They are not very friendly. Kind of scary, in fact."

He lifted his trunk up again until the rubbery tip reached the Fun House roof. Leroy turned and hugged it goodbye. Then we ran down a nearby ladder and joined up again with Finnigan.

"Boy," Leroy said. "It's hard to imagine anybody that big thinking of himself as small!"

"I guess it's all relative," I said, thinking about how Tiny was gigantic to us but a pipsqueak to the other elephants in the circus.

"What?" Finnigan was only half-listening. "Who's a relative?"

"We're all relatives," explained Leroy. "One big circus family."

"That's not what I meant," I shouted. "It's about **size**, you silly goose!"

"Yup, we all come in different sizes," Finnigan chimed in as we walked.

"That's not what it means." I wanted to pull my hair out.

"What **what** means?" asked Leroy.

"That it's all relative!!" I jumped up and down to emphasize the point.

"Like I said, we're all relatives," said Leroy with a happy smile.

"Gaaaaaahhhhhhh!!!!!!" I screamed in frustration...and then surrendered.

Then Leroy stopped and sniffed the air. "Do you smell that?"

Finnigan and I sniffed as well. The air was full of so many new smells to go with the amazing sights, but there was something familiar and pungent and dreamlike to the aroma. It smelled like the King of Beasts wagon.

A sound arose from just a few feet away that was a cross between a cough and a big truck starting up. Every hair stood up on my back, but Finnigan had finally found his destination.

Leroy took my hand and we both gulped. We were about to enter the lions' den!

Chapter Eight

THE LIONS' DEN

It wasn't hard to stay out of sight when we made our way inside. You couldn't possibly look at anything but the big cats lounging, napping, and in general just looking enormous and fearsome.

The big cats had all eyes on Finnigan, who had settled in to a cozy seat just outside a large cage containing a very large lion.

There was a shiny gold plate on the front of the cage that labeled this guy as "Nero." Something about where the cage was positioned made it seem like he was "top cat." Finnigan and Nero were deep in conversation already.

"Will you look at that," said Leroy, his eyes big as buttons. "That is a **lot** of lions."

Yes, it certainly was. I counted noses, and came up with three tigers, two jaguars, and a total of five lions. They all had paws like sledgehammers, and there were many white fangs on display as they gnawed on large bones and other enormous cat toys.

Finnigan looked absolutely starstruck. And why wouldn't he be? The big cats were legends to us all.

Leroy gave my ribs a dig and pointed to a spot just beyond Finnigan. Uh-oh.

Finnigan was not the only house cat in the tent. If you could call Finnigan a house cat at all. Well now we finally knew where Hector was. He had taken a seat just behind Finnigan, lurking off to the side but still in the circle of conversation. Trouble certainly came in twos.

On the other side of the bars, holding court, was an enormous lion that looked every inch as big and ferocious as the largest lions on the posters in the barn.

His nose was as wide as Finnigan's head. His mane looked like the pelt of a grizzly bear. His paws were the size of hams.

He scratched at his left ear with a hind foot attached to a leg that was as big and sturdy as a log. He winced, a face that scrunched his eyes and exposed his side, chewing teeth. Then he put the foot back down and resumed his Sphinx-like position of epic importance.

Nero glanced at us and wordlessly acknowledged us with an eyebrow shrug.

"And where are you both from?" Nero asked, speaking to Finnigan and Hector in a voice like a gravel truck at the bottom of a cave.

Finnigan sat up a little straighter. "I live in the Farnsworth Circus Museum here in town," he said proudly.

"So you are a circus cat?" Nero asked with an amused twinkle in his eyes. Finnigan nodded enthusiastically.

"And what of you, my dour-faced

friend?" Nero turned his attention to Hector. "Are you also in the circus?"

"Hardly," Hector sneered and spat. "I have a real **home**."

"So you are a soft and pampered house cat, then," Nero said with a slight sneer. "In such luxurious circumstances, it must be so…"

Hector narrowed his eyes and twitched his tail, expecting a compliment. "…**boring**," Nero finished. Hector's eyes widened at this put-down, but he wisely bit back a snappy comeback. I think he calculated roughly how far and how fast Nero could reach one of those giant paws through the metal bars.

"Kerchew!!" Leroy suddenly sneezed, and all eyes—Finnigan's, Hector's, Nero's and those of a half dozen other big cats—were suddenly on us. We felt like bugs under a magnifying glass.

Leroy waved nervously and cleared his throat. I didn't move a muscle. Or even a hair.

"Friends of yours?" Nero asked, shifting his gaze from Finnigan and Hector to Leroy and me, back and forth, back and forth.

"Oh yes," said Finnigan. "Family, in fact."

Leroy and I nodded wordlessly.

"They should be a meal," Hector said with a sneer.

"A meal, you say!" Nero laughed, a big, booming sound, then scratched his ear again and winced. "How can such a difference of opinion be between two creatures who are so alike?"

"We're not alike at all," Hector hissed. "This...*freak*...has turned his back on what it means to be a cat."

"Like us, do you think?" A pile of shadows came to life in the cage next to Nero's. He spoke with a Russian accent.

Orange and black stripes rearranged themselves into a huge tiger who lurched closer to the conversation. He smoothed his long, white whiskers with a gigantic pink tongue. I wondered whether it was a habit or meant that he was hungry.

"Boris, my friend and brother," Nero said, "I was wondering when you would join our philosophical conversation."

Nero addressed Finnigan and Hector. "Boris is a Siberian Tiger," he said. "His ancestors were feared throughout empires, and hunted by the Russian czars for sport. His ego can be a little inflated because of his pedigree, but you will not find a smarter or more learned tiger in all of the circus kingdom."

"That is so very true," Boris nodded in agreement.

"And we were discussing the notion of being brothers 'under the skin'," Nero said. Both big cats fixed their gaze on Hector. "And how does this...brother...of yours stray from the path of the cat?"

"He doesn't eat mice," Hector spat. "He **lives** with them. He's **friends** with them," he added as though it was the worst insult he could think of.

Finnigan's eyes narrowed and the tip of his tail started to jerk, a sure sign that this was getting under his skin.

Nero turned to him. "And what say you, my friend?" Then another scratch, another uncomfortable wince, another shake of that bear-like mane.

Leroy and I both edged closer to Finnigan, keeping him between us and Hector. The movement caught Nero's eye.

Before Finnigan could speak, Leroy piped up, clearly caught up in the moment.

"Finnigan is in our family," he said proudly. "He saved my life once...heck, more than once...and so we're as close a family as you'll ever find," he said. One thing you can say about Leroy, he wears his heart on his sleeve. If he wore sleeves.

"Did this rescue possibly involve our friend over there with the face pinched in unpleasantness?" Nero nodded at Hector.

"He should have been eaten long ago," Hector hissed angrily.

"I see," said Nero.

Finnigan smiled. "You step up for family," he said. "It's only natural!" I got a lump in my throat. Boy, we'd taught the kid well! Leroy looked from Finnigan and back to Nero.

"He is **really** brave, your honor," he said, and then proceeded to tell Nero the entire adventure. He started with how he'd been trying to balance on a cable between the house and the barn while carrying too many walnuts, and ended with Finnigan flying through the air to snatch him from the jaws of doom while Hector and Godfrey waited hungrily below.

Hector looked as though his head was going to explode.

Nero scratched his ear again, and Boris edged closer to the front of his cage.

"So you think we are defined by what we eat," Boris said. "That you are not a cat if you do not eat mice?"

Boris stared at Hector, but with all those stripes on his face, it was hard to read his expression.

Hector nodded. "Yes." I thought I saw a corner of drool form on his skinny lips.

"And what about us?" Boris said with an undercurrent of challenge. He drew himself up to his full height, stripes echoing bamboo in a forest of lights and shadows, warmth deceptively radiating off that soft fur.

Hector calculated the distance between Boris and himself, and inched backwards a little before answering.

"You should be the one to talk," he sneered. "Look at what has become of you."

Both Boris' and Nero's formidable eyebrows shot up at that.

"You look down on me for a life of comfort, but do you kill what you eat?" Hector continued. "Just look at where you live…in a box!"

"Watch yourself, my friend," Boris said, "or I will use your skinny legs as toothpicks." Hector backed up another step and reflexively looked over his shoulder. "We are not doing anything we do not want to do," Boris added.

Hector rolled his eyes, but Boris pressed his point. "We play and work together, as a family. Our trainer—Miss Gloria—knows that any of us could eat her if we wished. But we are a team, and kindness goes a long way toward making that happen."

"Kindness," Hector spat the word out. "When are cats supposed to be kind? Your 'kind' is famous for being bloodthirsty and cruel."

"Yes, it is true, we have earned our lofty reputations," Boris said. "My great grandfather ate twenty peasants one summer just for sport. He was feared up and down the range of the Ural Mountains until the Cossacks finally caught him. His hide was on display for decades in the Winter Palace in Russia."

"Oh don't go claiming all the glory,"

Nero said. "If we're going to keep score, my grandmother ate an entire village in the Nile delta. **And**, to her credit, she was never caught. But times have changed, my elegantly striped friend."

Boris shook his head, a big cat's version of a shrug. The stripes were like an optical illusion, and he seemed to disappear for just a second. I felt a little dizzy.

"Did you see that?" I reached over to nudge Leroy in the ribs, but my elbow met thin air.

Chapter Nine

OPPOSITES ATTRACT

I've mentioned that Leroy can move pretty quickly when wants to, and for some reason he had scaled the top of Nero's head and was holding on to his hairy ear with both hands.

Nero suddenly froze. I thought my

own heart would stop.

Leroy twisted his head this way and that, as though inspecting the best approach to detaching a ripe apple from Old Man Farnsworth's tree. Then he dove in as though he was going to bite Nero on the ear.

The shock brought me to my knees. Clearly Leroy was taking this whole lovey dovey circus family stuff a bit too much to heart. You just don't go pulling on a tiger's tail or biting a lion on the ear and expect to live to tell about it!

Nero cocked his head to the side and made as if to use his back paw again to scratch whatever had been bothering him, but suddenly stopped. The giant hind foot hovered in mid-air. Then Leroy came up for air holding a giant splinter in his teeth, and you could see Nero relax.

He heaved a contented sigh and tilted his head forward. "Thank you my little friend," he said. "I am in your debt."

Leroy just sat there with the goofiest grin on his face. Nero opened his front paw like a landing pad. "Come down here and visit," he said. "I promise no harm will come to you."

"Didn't anyone tell you that it's impolite to play with your food?" That was Hector on the sidelines, of course. "Go ahead and eat him. Somebody should!"

Finnigan looked at me and gave an amused shrug. He and Nero seemed to be on the same feline wavelength and it was a friendly one so far. I edged over to sit beside him. Leroy took Nero up on his invitation, and nestled into the giant paw, which curled around him like a furry fortress.

"And why would I eat something so incredibly brave?" mused Nero. He stroked the top of Leroy's head, and Leroy happily leaned into it.

"Brave," Hector spat again. "More like foolhardy. Careless. Stupid."

Nero seemed quite absorbed in the sight of Leroy in his paw, and Boris took up the mantle of spokes-cat.

"Bravery, indeed it is," he said with that luxurious Russian accent. Hector looked at him from under a furrowed brow.

"To save someone, to help someone, that you love," he continued. "That is easy. But as your little friend here has demonstrated, to risk helping someone that you do not know, now ***that*** is a very different story. And clearly, you have not heard it before."

"Heard what?" asked both Hector and Finnigan together.

Boris rolled his eyes. "Evidently, your education in the classics has been lacking," he said. "Do you not agree that we should expand their knowledge, my brother?" he asked, and Nero nodded.

"Very well," Boris said. "I will not bore you with extra flourishes, but there was once a great and powerful Lion. He was King of the Jungle and all that he surveyed. One day he was napping in his favorite clearing, and a Mouse ran across his head."

"The Lion reached up and snatched the mouse with a giant paw." I gulped at this point and looked over at Leroy nestled in Nero's paw. Leroy was absolutely transfixed. "He regarded the Mouse with curiosity. 'Why did you wake me from my nap?' he asked the small creature who trembled with fear in his hand."

"The Mouse answered that he had been fleeing from a hungry Fox, and begged the Lion to spare his life."

"Any why should I do that?" asked the Lion. "I am rather hungry right now. And I have eaten other animals with much less provocation."

"I can think of no reason," the Mouse said, "but please don't. I will be forever in your debt."

"The Lion laughed at the Mouse's suggestion that he could possibly help such a powerful entity as himself, but he let the Mouse go free anyway and then went back to sleep."

"A few days later the Lion was walking through the jungle with all the confidence of a King when he was suddenly snared in a net of rope and found himself hanging from a tree branch above the jungle floor."

"Despite his size and strength, he was helpless to free himself, and he knew that it was just a matter of time before the hunters who had set this trap returned to claim their prize. The Lion felt that all was lost. But then who should show up at the scene but the very Mouse whose life he had spared. The Mouse could have continued on his way but instead he ran up the tree and down to the net of rope. After studying the net from all angles, he began to gnaw through the rope with his tiny teeth until the net gave way and the Lion was free."

"I thank you for your kindness," said the Lion. "But why did you help me?"

"Kindness is never wasted," said the Mouse, and he scurried back into the jungle.

For the next few seconds, we all sat very, very quietly, letting the pictures that Boris had painted in our heads sink in. Though one look at Hector's face made it clear that Boris' storytelling had failed at reaching his better nature.

"I don't get it," he said. "That's got nothing to do with being brave."

Boris sighed. "It is a variation on a theme," he said, "where the essentials of kindness, courage, honor, and loyalty all converge in one body of thought. But I fear that you are unteachable about these things."

Nero seemed to beckon to Finnigan and Hector with his other paw. "Come closer, my miniature cousin," he said.

"Me?" asked Finnigan, eagerly leaning forward.

"No, him," Nero cocked a shaggy eyebrow at Hector.

Hector slinked forward, scowling, his belly rubbing the ground and his dark, skinny tail trailing behind.

He stopped when he was nearly nose to nose with Leroy.

"I know what you are thinking," Nero said. "You think that this is a neutral zone of sorts, a place where all of us can converse without giving in to our natural tendencies, shall we say. But that once you have left this tent, the mice here will again be fair game."

There was an ugly flicker in Hector's icy blue eyes. Nero had nailed it.

"We are not all that different under the skin," Nero continued. But there was something in his tone that made me think that he wasn't quite finished.

"This tiny creature has gone outside of his usual role of meekness and timidity and bravely done me a kindness," he said. He gave Leroy a nudge with the tip of his broad nose. "And Elephants are not the only animals in the circus with long memories."

Hector looked like he was going to barf.

"Well excuse me your worship," he said, "but yes, you're right. Outside this tent, these mice—and especially this fat one you evidently are so fond of—are mine." He flicked at one of the iron bars with a claw, then jumped back out of reach.

"You are mistaken," Nero replied calmly, but his voice dropped to a low and dangerous rumble. "My reach here, you see, stretches far beyond this cage. Far beyond this tent, in fact."

Hector and Finnigan and I all turned around right then to look—we couldn't help ourselves.

"Do not think that you will not be watched...or brought back to me from any distance to answer if they are harmed."

Hector might have dared to say more but a bright beam of daylight suddenly lit up the doorway as Boomer pushed his way inside. I was so happy to see the big lug I could have kissed him! Hector wisely kept his distance.

"That's our ride," Leroy said, as he clambered out from Nero's paw and then out of the cage. As we waved the last part of our goodbyes, I caught a glimpse of Nero's eyes reflecting like golden discs in the shadows. I was so glad that he was on our side.

Chapter Ten

ANTICIPATION!!

When the sun went down and the moon and stars came out, the Farnsworth house was finally quiet. Finnigan and Leroy and I hung out in the hay loft, listening to the sounds of circus music and laughter floating on the breeze from the fairgrounds. The circus might not be performing tonight, but that didn't mean that half the town wasn't enjoying the Midway already.

Carnival barkers were inviting folks to "step right up" and throw baseballs at a stack of milk bottles; fish for goldfish in a plastic pond; and spend money in every direction to win stuffed animals that ranged from the size of Leroy to as big as Boomer.

The Midway was also full of hot dogs, and cotton candy, and popcorn with caramel coating, and so the breeze smelled like a banquet disguised as a picnic.

Leroy had found some sunflower seeds by the bird feeder in the yard, and he cracked them open, one at a time, slowly chomping on their soft insides with a thoughtful air. There's rarely a time when Leroy isn't eating—or at least thinking about eating—and the soft, rhythmic "crunch, crunch" was like a lullaby.

Finnigan rested his elbows on the window sill and looked out at the halo of light over the fairgrounds. It had been a long day, but every hair on him from his nose to his tail was still wide awake. "I don't know about you guys," he said, "but I don't know how I'm going to sleep tonight!"

"You could try counting sheep," I offered.

"Ha!" said Finnigan. "Do you see any sheep around here?"

He had a point.

"Try counting fireflies," said Leroy. "It

always works for me."

"Oh, why not," Finnigan said with a sigh. We joined him on the sill and leaned over, watching the little yellow lights flicker in the grass and the flower beds.

"How do they do that?" I wondered out loud.

"Magic?" said Leroy. This was almost always his go-to line of thinking.

The fireflies sparkled and glowed as we watched. It was like staring at stars twinkling, but under us instead of above us.

A sudden swirl of air lifted one of the fireflies up the side of the barn, and then deposited him on the window sill. We all held our breaths so as not to frighten the little guy. Tiny legs wiped down his antennas for a good long while, and a wing fluffed into a better position. Then with barely a hop of a launch, he was airborne again and twinkling away into the distance.

Leroy was already working on another sunflower seed. I snuck a glance over at Finnigan. He was spellbound, looking into the dark where our little visitor had vanished and trying to pick him out from the crowd of sparkling lights in the yard.

"That was one high-flying bug!" he said with amusement.

Just like Finnigan was one unexpectedly high-flying cat, I thought. I glanced over my shoulder as I snuggled back into the hay for my beauty sleep. I was super tired, and didn't need to count **anything** in order to fall asleep.

A streak of moonlight reflected off the trapeze bar hanging above the ring. As I drifted off to sleep, I had the funny feeling that even though we'd scratched Finnigan's itch to meet up with his big circus cat cousins, we weren't quite done with adventuring. After all, he was a cat that could ***fly!***

There was a whole 'nuther world of excitement waiting for us tomorrow. I was absolutely sure of it.

Chapter Eleven

UNDER THE BIG TOP!!

The three of us hitched a ride to the circus the next morning in the Farnsworth minivan when nobody was looking. At least nobody that could talk!

Shirley had left the side door open

after she buckled Mikey into his car seat and then rounded up the rest of the family. The plan was for Finnigan to hide behind the spare wheel on the back as the van started up, and for Leroy and me to sneak under the middle seat when nobody was looking. Boomer looked on with sad, lonesome eyes from his perch on the porch.

"Pull your tail in a little farther," I told Leroy as we settled in to a spot just under Mikey's seat. All we needed was for that boy to figure out how to say "mouse" this morning, and we'd ***all*** be in a world of trouble!

Leroy harrumphed, like he was offended at the thought that he didn't know how to make himself invisible, but then reached out for a candy wrapper a few inches away.

"Do you think there's anything in here?" he said, sniffing with optimism. The crinkled plastic rustled as he pulled on it. I slapped his hand away. Out of the corner of my eye, I could see Mikey crane his neck to look in our direction.

"I'm hungry!" Leroy said with a scowl.

"You're always hungry!" I shot back. "Just wait 'til we get there."

Leroy folded his arms and sulked, the very picture of wounded dignity.

Compared with riding on Boomer's back, the trip to the fairgrounds went amazingly fast. We all darted away from the minivan as soon as Fred parked it, and then Finnigan and Leroy and I snuck in to the Big Top through a ripped seam in one of the canvas tent walls.

Outside had been plenty busy, with little stands and rope corrals set up for kids to get elephant rides and pony rides; pet a camel and a llama and a tiny donkey close up; or get their faces painted to look like circus animals. So far the lions and tigers were winning that popularity contest.

But inside was where the magic would happen, and so we didn't linger outside for long.

"Holey Moley," said Finnigan once the last of his tail cleared the canvas.

"Yeah," said Leroy.

For twice now in a blue moon, I didn't have anything to add. So ***this*** was what had caused Great-Great-Great-Great Grandpa Felix to dart out of the doctor's vest pocket and into the arms of adventure and excitement, turning all of us in the family that followed into circus mice from ears to tails.

What a ***spectacle!!*** The giant blue and red circus tent could have held three of the Farnsworth's barns inside it. We found a seat under the wooden bleachers where we could see all three rings lined up, with the biggest one in the middle. The sawdust made Leroy sneeze.

A large cage with metal bars and a safety net around the top occupied the ring on the far side of the tent, primed for the arrival of the big cats. At the other end, a pair of elephants with feathered head gear practiced balancing on tiny stools.

In the center ring, the Ringmaster paced around as the orchestra tuned up. He wore tall black boots and white breeches, and occasionally flicked dust off the fancy lapels of his bright red jacket. High above, a tightrope ran between two poles, and trapeze bars hung askew from some ***really*** tall ladders.

Two ladies in shimmering silver costumes with gossamer wings spun in lazy circles above us, hanging from ropes that dangled from the scaffolding at the top.

They looked like fairies covered with diamond dust. I was about to nudge Leroy in the ribs and remind him that fairies weren't actually real...and then reconsidered. I mean, he still believed in Mermaids. Why spoil things?

Clowns in gigantic shoes passed us by, while poodles wearing silver hats and matching capes scampered every which way underfoot.

"Popcorn, get yer popcorn," sang out a skinny teenager in a white uniform as he walked up and down the bleachers with a tray full of paper bags spilling over with the crunchy stuff. Other teens hawked sodas and hot dogs and balloons.

Finnigan stretched up to his full height and peered over a higher row of bleacher seats. "I see the Farnsworths over there," he said, pointing with a paw. "Might be a good idea to stick close to them," he said.

It turned out that the Farnsworths, being the owners of the local circus museum, were seated with Beechville's mayor and few other high and mighty townsfolk in premium seats right in front of the center ring.

Seeing over the ring wasn't going to be a problem for Finnigan, but mice are not known for size. Okay, maybe Leroy is, but even he was going to have trouble. Finnigan found an empty cardboard box and put it right under the Farnsworths' seats.

"This view is terrific," Finnigan said as he looked out between Charlie's feet.

"It sure is," said Leroy, though his eyes were focused on a big cloud of pink cotton candy that Lucy held in one hand. She had a box of popcorn under her other elbow, and as she reached from one side to the other, popcorn rolled over the side to land at our feet.

I was about to tell Leroy to pay more attention, when the tent suddenly went black. We heard the sounds of feet, big and small, shuffling in front of us as folks in the audience waited for their eyes to adjust to the darkness.

And then a beam of light lit up the center ring, gleaming off the gold trimmings on the Ringmaster's jacket, and he held up his microphone. In a booming voice he said the words that Leroy and Finnigan and I had only heard of in bedtime stories...

"Ladies and Gentlemen, Children of All Ages, Welcome to The Spence-Haywaller Circus!!"

Chapter Twelve

THE SHOW BEGINS!!

As the Ringmaster spoke, the band began to play and spotlights swung around the tent.

"The Elephants!" Leroy said, as a line of six giant pachyderms filed into the center ring. They wore fantastic head pieces and fancy bracelets that jingled and jangled around their huge ankles.

"Look, there's Tiny!" said Finnigan. Yep, it was our rescuer from the day before. The silver and pink ostrich feathers in his headpiece perfectly matched his freckles. Tiny brought up the rear, looking quite a bit smaller than his cousins. He was still bigger than the minivan we'd arrived in.

The elephant trainer, Miss Sadie, rode in on the first of the elephants in line. She was a tiny lady in a shiny pink and gold costume, and she worked those gentle giants like they were dancers in a ballet.

They sat on their haunches, with their trunks up in the air and their front feet up, looking like puppies begging for treats. They stood on their front feet, with their saggy bottoms in the air. They balanced like trained seals on tiny stools, and then balanced on each other, making an elephant pyramid of wrinkly grey skin and sequins.

And at the very end, the biggest elephant curled his trunk around Miss Sadie and lifted her up in the air and then to the top of his head. Then he reared up like a horse, and Miss Sadie whistled, and all six filed back into line to trot around the ring like trick ponies.

"Wow," said Leroy. "I never knew something so big could be so...graceful!" I had thought the very same thing, though I usually don't tell him when that happens. It's like it would upset the balance of the universe or something. But yes, "grace" was the very word. Up close, their size was just overwhelming, but from a distance, they nearly floated between steps. Appearances could be so deceiving!!

When they finally lumbered out of the ring, the crowd gave a roar of applause. That instantly turned into laughter when the next act rolled in, a pony cart carrying two small dogs dressed in lion costumes, from shaggy manes down to the tufts on their tails.

"I wonder if Nero and Boris know about this," Finnigan mused as the seats above us shook with giggling kids and grownups.

Accompanied by a clown with rainbow hair and polka dot pants, they did a pint-sized version of a lion act, all leaps and somersaults and balancing and jumping through hoops. It was a great imitation. If it wasn't for the barking and the tail wagging, they'd have been dead ringers for little lions!!

They all took their bows, and the tent suddenly went dark again. Fancy patterns of light swirled across the floor, and music began, something delicate and classical, a Viennese Waltz. A shivery snort broke the lilting rhythm.

"What the heck could this one be?" asked Leroy, as all three of us peered into the blackness.

"Horses," said Finnigan. Of course, those green cat eyes of his could see just about anything.

And then, into the empty ring galloped six horses that had to be the most beautiful animals I had ever imagined.

Three of them were coal black, and

three were white that shone like silver. They wore no saddles, no halters, no bridles, no fancy feathers. Their long, wavy manes hung nearly to their knees, and their tails flowed like silk behind them.

They reared and circled together, and then split into two streams of light and dark, trotting and spinning and prancing and weaving through and past each other without a single polished hoof put wrong. They were power and poetry in motion.

Their trainer stood in the center of the ring, her long blond hair flowing down her back like the horses' tails, over a gown of gleaming silver. She held a long, skinny whip in each hand that she used like a symphony conductor with a baton.

"Look at that," said Leroy. "It reminds me of watching Old Man Farnsworth fly fishing in the stream behind the house!"

"Shhhh...." I said and nudged him in the ribs.

"What's with you?" Finnigan asked. "It's not like you haven't seen liberty horses on the posters in the barn before this."

I held a finger up to my lips and just kept staring. As far as I was concerned, this was a close to pure magic as you could get.

"If you watch closely," said Finnigan, "you can see that she's giving them signals with those whips, even if she's not touching them."

"Shhhh..." I said again. Finnigan and Leroy gave me funny looks, and then shrugged it off.

I didn't care. I didn't want to know how this all worked. I didn't want to think about how these horses knew what to do next, or how they managed to look like they were **_dancing_** to the music. For the first time in my short, circus mouse life, I was as spellbound as Leroy imagining fairies hanging from the rigging at the top of the tent, lost in the music and the movement.

In all of those bedtime stories about how Great-Great-Great-Great Grandpa Felix had been overcome with emotion and wonder when his owner walked into a circus in Berlin, and then darted away into the circus life then and there, nobody had ever said exactly what it was that had captured his eye and his heart with such force.

Was it the aerialists flying above on the trapeze? The lions leaping through circles of flame? The elephants walking past in all their majestic and exotic glory?

No one really knew or remembered.

The horses finished their graceful movements and bowed their heads over bended knees as the crowd applauded, then left the ring as the spiraling patterns followed and gleamed off their flowing manes and tails.

And as I stared after them in the dark, I knew for absolutely certain that if I'd been in Felix's shoes...okay, in the royal physician's vest pocket...and I saw those liberty horses prancing and twirling and galloping in the ring, that would have been "it" for me.

Chapter Thirteen

INTERMISSION

The regular lights went on and the spotlights went off, and the Ringmaster announced that it was time for Intermission.

Kids thundered down the bleachers dragging their parents behind them, and raced toward the exits to get in another pony ride or face painting that they missed before, or maybe even kiss a camel.

The Farnsworths were right in step, as Lucy lobbied to get her face painted like a unicorn, and Charlie angled for an elephant ride. Mikey was still too small to get a vote in these proceedings, so Shirley scooped him up in her arms and suddenly we had the place to ourselves.

Mikey dropped both his caramel popcorn and the cotton candy in the excitement. Shirley gave them a quick backward glance and then, seeing just how much sawdust they'd landed in, wrinkled her nose and gave him a quick kiss before continuing to herd her brood out of the tent.

Finnigan was so excited his fur nearly

lifted off his back. "I'm going to walk around," he said. "Want to come with?"

Leroy had just managed to drag the box of caramel corn to a safer spot under the bleachers, and looked up, his mouth full of sweet and sticky goodness. "Mmmmmph," he said, shaking his head and pointing to his chin.

I translated, which I often do when food is involved. "I'm pretty sure that means 'no'," I said. Plus, I was ready to stay put. Everything was so much farther for us than for Finnigan!

Finnigan didn't stick around to argue, but I noticed that he still stayed undercover, keeping to the shadows and lurking under the seats. Good habits are hard to break.

"Here, give me some of that," I said, and Leroy handed me a piece of caramel corn. It was buttery, and sweet, and absolutely heavenly when it crunched.

Then I pulled off a tuft of pink cotton candy, and twirled it into a moustache. "What do you think?" Leroy laughed so hard a piece of corn hit me in the chest. Then he grabbed a bigger fluffy piece, and modeled on his head like a wig. Ah, life was good!!

Despite the tent being littered with snacks all around us still waiting to be discovered, Leroy was determined to get the last pieces inside the box.

"It's not safe," I hissed. People were already starting to walk back into the tent.

"But the best part is at the bottom," Leroy argued. "There's extra sauce in the corners."

There was no talking him out of it,

and the box rustled in the sawdust as Leroy tugged and tugged at a particularly tempting piece of popcorn stuck to the bottom.

Then the lights started to dim and the band began to play again.

"Get out of there," I said, "***now!!***" But it was too late.

The Farnsworths plopped themselves down in their seats just as the Ringmaster welcomed everybody back for the second half of the show. Mikey, who absolutely never sat still if squirming was an option, turned around, looked under his seat, and picked up the box of caramel corn he'd left behind.

The box of popcorn that still had Leroy inside it.

The box of popcorn that Mikey looked into just as one of those spotlights landed on the front row and lit up the Farnsworth family like they were sitting in church at Easter.

And that's exactly when Mikey saw Leroy inside the box and then shouted "***MOUSE!!***" as clear as day.

Well, the kid finally got his brain and his words to work together! I thought I'd have a heart attack from the fright any second, and imagined that the shock to Leroy had to be ten times worse.

Mikey held the popcorn box up to Shirley with two hands, and kept yelling that darned "mouse" word over and over again at the top of his lungs, like he'd invented electricity or something.

Shirley took the box from him, sort of absent mindedly because her attention was more on the family of jugglers performing in the center ring. But when she looked down and saw Leroy, she gave a little scream and nearly threw the box in the air.

What a pickle we were in! All that **time**, all that **work**, all that **secrecy!**

Hiding in the crevices and the woodwork of the house. Sneaking inside through tiny holes and cracks, and crossing over from the barn on tree branches and power cables. All that being "quiet as a mouse" as we came and went in the house and the barn, leaving no traces that we were ever there.

And then to have our cover blown **right here**, right in the front row of the circus!!

If Leroy made it out of this mess alive, I thought, we were definitely going to have to find someplace else to live. And if he didn't, well...it was going to be pretty darn lonely in that barn, even with Finnigan for company. Mice aren't meant to be loners.

Shirley elbowed Fred to get his attention. Fred, who had been watching the lions enter the cage to the right, looked back at Shirley, who handed him the box without another word.

Fred looked inside and laughed. "Oh honey, it's a mouse!!" Oh, poor Leroy!

"Mikey found him in the popcorn box," Shirley said. "What do you think we should we do with him?"

What, did she think that the circus might have some Mouse Police waiting by the exits?

Fred set the box down on the floor beneath his seat, with the opening toward the back of the bleachers. He gave it a little shake. Leroy stubbornly held on.

"I'm sure he's just a circus mouse," Fred said. "They probably have quite a few of them here, with all the food for the animals and the treats that land on the ground."

A circus mouse? My mind reeled. Had Fred been on to us the whole time?

"I'm sure he'll find his way back to where he came from," he continued. He shook the box a little harder until Leroy tumbled out in a confused and terrified muddle.

"I'll bet he's got a nice little nest with a few friends in one of the feed trucks," he said and sighed. "What a way to see the country!!"

"Over here," I hissed, beckoning a quivering Leroy to get the heck out of view. He lumbered over, sawdust sticking to the gooey caramel on his paws.

Fred put the empty box on the ground by his feet and signaled for the popcorn vendor to keep the stuff coming. Leroy plopped down beside me, and wiped a paw across his brow. Sawdust stuck to that too. Both our hearts were racing like crazy.

"I thought I was a goner for sure," Leroy said. I'd thought so too, but didn't pile it on.

I wondered where Finnigan had gotten himself to. The acrobats gathered their rings and chairs and hoops and jogged out of the center ring, and we could hear the sudden sound of a tiger's cough in the darkness.

Even though the big cats were friendly yesterday, the sound still sent a shiver down my spine! Then there was a louder roar, from Nero, and the spotlights rained down on the big cats.

Five lions and two leopards and three gigantic Siberian tigers sat on stools around the rim, snarling and pawing the air as their trainer—Miss Gloria, a dainty lady barely as tall as Charlie—took a bow. Dressed in bright turquoise satin and gold braid, she smiled as though she was in the safest place in the world...and then cracked her whip signaling that the show was about to start.

Lions leaped! Tigers balanced on giant balls, on ropes, on each other! The jaguars fetched and carried like retrievers! Miss Gloria brought out a giant hoop and set it on fire, then gestured to Nero. Nero sat up on his haunches, pawing at the air, showing off his enormous fangs, roaring like a train engine in a tunnel.

The sound echoed from one end of the tent the other, a rumbling, scary sound that has struck terror in smaller animals since the dawn of time. Even after meeting him yesterday and finding out he had a soft spot for Leroy and Finnigan, the sound still made me tremble.

As the flames licked around the edge of the hoop and Nero held his moment of suspense—would he or wouldn't he make that leap?—I looked for Finnigan. Where had he gone? He was missing the most important part of the circus! Or was he?

Leroy tugged at my elbow and pointed. We'd dragged the cardboard box as far forward as we could under the Farnsworths' seats without Mikey seeing us again. While all eyes and most of the lights were on the ring with the big cats, a single beam shown on the area above the cage, where one of the trapeze artists had climbed to a tiny platform and stood like a statue.

And just below the platform, shrouded in shadow and hanging by a paw and a tail, was Finnigan.

Talk about getting the best seat in the house!!

Chapter Fourteen

FRIGHT IN FLIGHT

After Nero's flaming finale, the big cats' act drew to a close with the ferocious felines behaving more like kittens, crowding around Miss Gloria to get their ears scratched and shoulders rubbed.

"Would you look at that," remarked Leroy as he watched Boris rub the side of his face against her tiny hip. "Just like when Finnigan was a baby."

I confess I was pretty awestruck as well. With all the deep roars and the sharp claws and the big fangs and the dire warnings yesterday in the lions' tent, I hadn't guessed that Boris and Nero and their cohorts really had this kind of a softer side. You learn something new every day.

Leroy nudged me in the ribs and pointed toward the ceiling with a broken piece of a peanut. Now where'd he get that, I wondered?

I looked up, and saw that the Flying Florentinos had finished their warm ups and were now embracing the spotlight as the new center of attention.

A man and a dark-haired girl, dressed head to toe in sparkly white and gold, stood on the tiny platform at one side of center ring, while a second man stood on the platform on the other side of the ring.

They "chalked up," dusting their palms in powdered white chalk that wafted upward in tiny plumes in the spotlight. They each raised an arm in a graceful salute to the crowd. Then the two men swooped confidently into the air, like hawks diving on a summer day. And believe me, as mice, Leroy and I certainly know what diving hawks look like!

As they swung back and forth in bigger arcs, we could see that one of the men hung from the bar from his knees, while the other one gripped the bar with his hands.

"One's the catcher," I told Leroy, "and

the other one's the flyer." I was recalling what Old Man Farnsworth would tell visitors at the circus museum on Sunday afternoons.

The flyer kept going higher and higher as he "kicked for the ceiling," and it seemed like he would soon hit the canvas top. Then as he arced back toward the catcher, he suddenly came loose and turned two somersaults in mid-air before his hands caught the arms of the catcher and the crowd quit holding their breaths.

"Wow," said Leroy. "It's just like watching Finnigan...except he doesn't need a catcher!"

I was pretty sure that having four feet and a tail had a lot to do with that fact, but Leroy was definitely right. If I had a crystal ball, I was sure it would predict that Finnigan would be doing even fancier aerial twists and turns when we all got back to the barn.

After several more gravity-defying exchanges, the flyer and the catcher briefly returned to their perches. Then the girl suddenly took to the air. She was mesmerizing. Sometimes she stood on the bar like a butterfly perched on a flower, sometimes she twisted and spun in mid-air between hand-offs like a dazzling jewel pendant on a necklace. You almost believed she had wings, because she sure could fly.

I felt, rather than saw, Leroy's attention swivel from the air to the ground, and I followed his gaze to where a large twist of pink cotton candy had fallen into the sawdust at the edge of the ring. After the incident with the caramel corn, he knew better than to try his luck with that, but as we both stared, Leroy looked a little farther and then sat up straighter.

"Where's the net?" he asked. "Aren't they supposed to have a net?"

I tried to remember anything Old Man Farnsworth might have said about nets and trapeze acts, but drew a blank.

"Maybe they don't always use them," I said.

"It's not like they're cats," he went on in worried fashion. "People don't always land on their feet."

"I'm sure they'll be fine," I tried to reassure him. Actually I didn't know that for sure, but it seemed like the right thing to say. I tried to recall if I'd seen any nets in the background of the circus posters in the barn, but I simply couldn't remember.

Leroy relaxed a little. He pointed up to he platform where we'd last seen

Finnigan. Finnigan wasn't there, but a grey and white speck on the rigging closer to the roof proved to be our favorite flyer, with an even better view of things from where he sat than before.

"Look," I told Leroy. "I think that the girl is getting ready to do something big." Like the first flyer had done, she was swooping in bigger and bigger arcs that reached nearer to the tent roof. It looked like she passed just inches from Finnigan on her last one.

And then two things happened at once. In the shadows of the rigging, we could see that Finnigan was suddenly on the move while the spotlight shone down on the airborne girl in white and gold.

And as the girl swung through the air as though she had wings, one side of the bar that she held came loose and she held fast to it with one hand as her other hand swung up to catch it. The audience gasped together. Our hearts were all in our throats for that long second as she hovered above the center ring, hoping that our wishes could keep her aloft.

And suddenly there was a streak of grey and white that crossed from the shadows through the light and back into the dark, just for an instant, and in that instant the girl suddenly had a rope in her other hand and the crowd went wild with cheers.

As she found her way back to the sawdust, the Ringmaster met her in the center ring and showed her off with a flourish as though the entire death-defying stunt had been planned all along.

Then the lights swung over to a set of acrobats in the far ring, and the audience's attention dutifully followed. Except for mine and Leroy's. We looked at each other.

"Where's Finnigan?" Leroy asked, and there was genuine fear in his eyes. "I can't see where he landed. What do you think happened?" he said, and he wrung his tail between his hands with anxiety.

"I'm sure he's fine," I said. That seemed to be my role in these situations, and I wasn't going to change that now. "He's a cat," I said, "and you know that they always land on their feet."

"I know," Leroy said, but his eyes were still big. "But I'd feel better if I could see him."

"Don't go anywhere until we figure out how it's safe to get there," I warned, and we both cast our eyes around the far side of the ring, looking for some sign of

Finnigan. "He'll stay where it's dark," I said.

Leroy tried to calm his nerves, as much for me as for himself. I appreciated it.

"Yeah, I wouldn't be surprised if he was sneaking up behind us right now," he said with a little laugh. It sounded forced, but it was still a good thing.

The audience laughed and applauded as the acrobats leaped and balanced, and the big cats lined up in the darkness to head for the exit.

It's a fact that animals sense things faster than people. Despite the music and the noise from the crowd, Leroy and I could hear whispers racing among the four-legged performers from one end of the tent to the other.

A cat had saved the day. Who was he?

Nobody knew. He had to be a stranger. This was a mystery. If he was a stranger, why did he do this? And where had he disappeared to?

Then another whisper, and another. He had been hurt, someone said. No, the stranger was fine, said someone else. They had seen him walk away. No, that wasn't true. No, he wasn't. Yes he was! One of the horses saw the whole thing before they left the tent. The stranger didn't look like he was moving from where he had fallen.

Leroy and I looked at each other, frozen in place in this swirl of rumor and whispers, hoping that only the good parts of the reports were true.

And then as one voice, Nero, Boris and the rest of the cats stopped in their tracks and let out a sorrowful roar that shook the tent to the very rooftops.

Leroy grabbed for my hand, and looked at me with big, worried eyes, and we both knew.

Finnigan hadn't landed on his feet.

Chapter Fifteen

A SURPRISE FINALE!!

If there's one really big theme in the history of the circus, it's that "the show must go on." It works, over and over again, because people are **really** easily distracted.

So the circus sure kept going on, right

above our heads, as Leroy and I sat under the Farnsworths' seats by the center ring. Laughter and applause alternated in waves as ponies pranced, and dogs did back flips, and more acrobats leaped and balanced, and clowns tripped over each other and everything else in sight. The trapeze artists took to the skies again, although the spot under the platform where Finnigan had been sitting was still empty.

It was just too big and busy and bustling a place for me and Leroy to think about trying to cross the tent without getting stepped on, or worse. Leroy's shoulder's sagged with sadness and uncertainty.

"We should get a head start now," I said. "Once the show is over, we'll never get to the car before the family leaves."

Leroy nodded slowly and took my hand as we walked cautiously between the food and the litter underneath the bleachers. For once, the thought of food meant absolutely nothing to him. Or me.

When we got to the canvas wall of the Big Top where we'd snuck in, we turned back for one last look. Leroy gave a giant, mournful sigh. I knew how he felt. This certainly wasn't the way we ever imagined a trip to the actual circus would end, even in our wildest dreams.

In the front row, the Farnsworths were still enjoying the magical night—Charlie, Lucy, Mikey sitting in Fred's lap. The spot next to Fred where Shirley had been sitting when she discovered Leroy was empty. She was probably getting another box of caramel corn, I figured, to replace the one she'd found with Leroy sitting inside.

As we stepped out of the tent and into the dark night, we ran smack into Boomer's big, loveable face. Leroy was so happy to see him he threw his arms around Boomer's muzzle, and I could feel gusts of wind coming off of his wagging tail. The big guy must been lonesome, sitting home by himself, and followed our scent right to the spot where we'd entered the tent earlier in the night.

Leroy and I climbed aboard and settled in on his broad shoulders. Boomer made as if to shove his head through the rip in the tent wall, but Leroy tugged at his ear to get his attention.

"We need to get home," he said. "We'll tell you all about what you've missed on the way."

The sounds from the Midway began to

fade as Boomer made his way through the tall grass like a ship under sail, and the dark settled all around us like a cloak.

We finally reached the Farnsworths' driveway with heavy hearts. Boomer suddenly jumped sideways into the ditch by the mailbox and out of range of the yard light.

"What the heck!" Leroy said, his fists gripping Boomer's yellow fur. As Boomer crouched lower and out of sight, a white van with fancy letters on the side stopped at the end of the driveway and checked for traffic from each direction before creeping forward into the road and heading toward the town.

There were lots of words on the side, but the word that had the biggest letters started with the letter "V."

"What do you think that meant?"

Leroy asked as the van's red taillights disappeared into the night. "Violins? Vertigo? Verisimilitude?"

I had to admit I was stumped as well. I thought I had a pretty good vocabulary, especially for a mouse, but all I could think of on the spot was "Vine" and "Velvet" and "Violets." And that van didn't seem like it belonged to a flower shop.

After the van left, Boomer heaved a sigh of relief and quit crouching. Then he shrugged his shoulders, our cue that the ride was over and it was time for us to part company again.

Boomer trotted around the side of the yard, keeping to the shadows, until he reached the front porch. Then with a leap and a turn, he settled into a spot by a potted geranium, his head resting on his paws, the absolute picture of innocence.

He looked as though he'd spent the entire evening in that spot, guarding the house. I guess everybody's got their secrets in this place!

The remaining distance across the yard was not very far at all, but Leroy pulled at my tail to keep me from going any farther.

"Hey, watch it there!" I said.

"Can't we just sit here a little longer?" he asked wistfully. Despite everything that had happened it certainly **was** a beautiful summer night, with a cool breeze and a clear black sky that sparkled with stars.

Some of the stars seemed to be moving, and one of them buzzed by Leroy's head. The fireflies were out in force again, and they danced among the flowers and grass like little jewels.

I remembered sitting in the barn just the night before with Finnigan and Leroy, watching the fireflies from above, and my heart hurt. Or maybe it was my stomach. Or both.

"You know," said Leroy, "maybe it'll all turn out okay."

I turned and looked at him, puzzled. "How do you mean?"

"Maybe we've just been worried for nothing," he said. "Maybe Finnigan made it back here before we did, and he's waiting in the barn to surprise us. You know how he loves to pounce!"

Leroy started to smile at the very thought, even though I could remember how his heart nearly stopped with fright the first time Finnigan tried out his "pounce" setting on us.

I hated to suggest that he was wrong.

But I knew in my heart that if it had been possible, Finnigan would never have left the Big Top without us.

The lightning bug that had buzzed by Leroy's head began to meander toward the barn, and I poked Leroy in the shoulder.

"Time to get back to the barn, buddy," I said, and we both started on the last leg of the walk home. The barn door was ajar by a few inches, and light spilled through the space from inside.

"Now that's kind of weird," I said. Leroy nodded. "Nobody should be home but Boomer and us."

We sidled along the side of the front door and peered inside. Both of our jaws dropped open in amazement.

It seemed that the surprises weren't quite over for the evening. Finnigan in fact **had** arrived home before us.

Our eyes adjusted in a few seconds from the dark to the light. The tip of Finnigan's long tail rested on the floor, but the rest of him was draped over somebody's lap. We could hear purring, loud and clear, which was a very good sign.

Leroy suddenly sucked in his breath and then pointed. Finnigan's left front paw was the only part of that leg that wasn't wrapped in white bandages. But he didn't seem uncomfortable at all.

As a matter of fact, as we watched, he purred even louder and stretched his face upwards, closing his big green eyes contentedly.

Shirley readjusted Finnigan's position on the blanket in her lap, and nuzzled his nose as she stroked his ears.

SHIRLEY?????

We were too dumbfounded to even twitch.

SHIRLEY????? She didn't look all that surprised.

We scratched our heads in unison. My mind flashed back to the biggest word on the sign on the white van we had seen leaving the yard just a few minutes earlier.

VETERINARIAN. A doctor for animals. Shirley must have seen Finnigan fall and gotten him out of there to safety. But...

SHIRLEY?????

And we had thought it was Mikey who had the sharpest eyes in the family!

Leroy was so happy to see Finnigan again that he started to launch himself across the floor until I grabbed him by the hand and yanked him back.

"Ow!!" he said as he fell back on his haunches. "Why'd you do that?"

"Finnigan might not be a secret around here," I said, "but that doesn't mean that the rest of the family knows about us. For all they know, after finding you in that box of caramel corn, they think you'll be on a circus truck out of town tonight!"

Further conversation was suddenly cut off by the sound of the minivan pulling into the yard. Doors opened and then slammed shut, and Fred and Lucy and Mikey and Charlie all poured in through the doorway.

"Hey honey," Fred said, "you really missed a great finale! They shot some guy out of a cannon!!" He stopped short to keep from tripping over the kids, who had basically stopped dead in their tracks when they saw Shirley and Finnigan all cozied up on a bale of hay.

Lucy's eyes were as big as saucers. As the old saying goes, "the cat was finally out of the bag."

Charlie looked pleasantly amazed to find that there was apparently a new pet in the family.

And Mikey was jumping for joy at finally being validated, alternating shouts of "**_FINNIGAN_**" and "**_MOUSE_**" over and over.

Leroy shrank back further into the shadows, and I did as well. "Do you think he knows where we are?" he asked nervously.

"He knows we're around, that's all that matters," I replied. "But at least Shirley and Fred think that you're still back at the circus!"

Lucy was the first of the kids to walk up to her mom's lap and stroke Finnigan's fur.

"Can I hold him?" she asked, worried about the broken leg.

Shirley scooched over on the bale and let Lucy get comfortable, then transferred Finnigan and the blanket to her daughter's lap.

"Cool!" said Charlie. "Can we keep him?"

Mikey just kept jumping and shouting. After all, Finnigan was no surprise to **him!!**

And then Fred started to sneeze. Over and over and over. He finally just parked his handkerchief on top of his nose.

Lucy looked up at Shirley, embarrassment written all over her face.

"When did you find out?" she asked

her mother sheepishly.

"Almost from the start," Shirley said and kissed the top of Lucy's head. "When I was your age I brought home a stray kitten and hid him in the garage for a week before my mom found out."

Fred looked up from saying "achoo" into his handkerchief and beetled his brows. "So that's why I've been sneezing so much out here," he said.

Shirley laughed. Lucy relaxed just a little bit, and Charlie once again pressed the point.

"So really, can we keep him?"

All eyes turned to Fred, who pinched his nose to stifle another sneeze. But it was Shirley who came up with a solution.

"Come on, honey," she said to Fred. "I know just how much this means to Lucy… and I've already been checking out allergy medicines for the past two months. I am **sure** that we'll find something that will let you hold Finnigan in your lap!!"

The look on Fred's face was pretty dubious...but then he brightened up and smiled.

"You know," he said, "this explains a lot. I'll bet I'll end up sneezing less than I already have been!" Then he backed out of the barn and headed back to the house, seemingly sneezing less with every step.

We watched the rest of the Farnsworths as they hovered around Finnigan and learned how Lucy had found him and first brought him home, wrapped up in a sweater in her bicycle basket.

Fred came back to retrieve Mikey and

get him started on a bath. Yes, after all that caramel corn, cotton candy and assorted sawdust, the kid would certainly need a rinse before bedtime.

Charlie fetched a bowl of milk and another of water from the house and brought it out to the barn. Then he rubbed Finnigan's head between the ears with his knuckles before leaving as well.

Finally, it was Shirley's turn. "Five more minutes," she told Lucy with a motherly wag of a finger. "I know you'll be back out here with him before the sun comes up!"

Lucy hugged Finnigan more tightly and rocked him back and forth, singing him a lullaby. Then she wrapped the blanket snugly around him against the cool of the night, and left, closing the barn door behind her.

At last we were alone!!

Leroy and I practically flew across the floor and pounced on our favorite cat.

"You're okay!" Leroy exclaimed between hugs.

"Yeah," Finnigan replied, his eyes half-closed with exhaustion, "though it was a little touch and go there for a while!"

"How did you get back here?" I asked as I nestled into the curve of his soft belly fur. "And for that matter, what the heck happened??"

"I was up on the rigging as that girl was swinging higher and higher on her trapeze bar," he said, "and on her last pass I could see that the bar was loose. I didn't even think before I jumped toward her with a rope. But I thought I'd have a better landing."

We all shuddered together.

"I don't know how," he added, "but Shirley was suddenly there, like she'd been watching me the whole time. And then the vet was patching me up, and you guys got here for the rest." He yawned with a great slowness, then settled in for a good night's sleep.

"Well you sure saved the day," Leroy said as he patted the fur in the crook of Finnigan's neck before picking the softest spot for his head. "Bravest thing I ever saw."

Finnigan was already asleep, and we weren't going to be far behind. I could feel a rumbling under me, though whether it was the sound of purring or snoring, I couldn't tell…and didn't care.

In just the past two days we'd gone to an actual circus, made friends with an elephant, met some really big cats, ridden a carousel, been discovered in the bottom of a popcorn box, and seen the stuff of family legends in the flesh. It was quite a set of discoveries, I thought.

But the most important one of all, I knew as I drifted off to sleep, was learning that our very own Finnigan had the heart of a lion.

Mary T. Wagner is an award-winning author, grandmother, and "cat mom" living in Wisconsin.

The idea for the Finnigan the Circus Cat stories was inspired by the combination of a real "rescue" kitten named Finnigan, and Mary's daughter who is a circus aerialist! Like his fictional namesake, the real Finnigan grew up to have long legs and a very long tail, and loved to pounce.

"Going to the circus has always been such a family treat!" Mary said. Her very favorite circus acts are the big cats and the liberty horses. While she has not yet ridden an elephant, she actually **has** kissed a camel!

Made in United States
Orlando, FL
07 November 2023

38661107R00091